The
Manager
Who Became an
Influencer

Harish Shivdasani works with business leaders, CEOs, senior management as well as high-potential senior executives to help them achieve greater leadership success, fulfil their life goals and create a unique identity in society. A former faculty of IIM Ahmedabad, he has published many papers and written two books on leadership and on the strategy for VUCA world.

Reach him at *www.shivdasani-lens.com*; *hksconsulting@gmail.com*

The
Manager
Who Became an
Influencer

Lessons in Leading and Mentoring

Harish Shivdasani

RUPA

Published by
Rupa Publications India Pvt. Ltd 2018
7/16, Ansari Road, Daryaganj
New Delhi 110002

Sales Centres:

Allahabad Bengaluru Chennai
Hyderabad Jaipur Kathmandu
Kolkata Mumbai

Copyright © Harish Shivdasani 2018

ISBN: 9788129149527

10 9 8 7 6 5 4 3 2 1

Printed at Repro Knowledgecast Limited, India

Contents

Preface

The performance of an organization and its departments, the loyalty of its members and the satisfaction they derive from belonging to the organization, and consequently, their tenure greatly depends on the way they are led and inspired by their superiors. Quite often, a member of an organization might continue in the company because of his superior, even if he has otherwise lost interest in the organization. Sometimes, it is because of the superior that a person might quit his job, even if he was otherwise interested in the organization. The superior-subordinate relationship, therefore, is crucial. In a way, every time a superior interacts with a subordinate, whether for a minute or for hours, he either motivates or demotivates him, at least to some extent. It is not really essential for the manager to have long sessions of mentoring and counselling with his people to improve their performance. In this book, I have suggested everyday interactive strategies that will help you to inspire and significantly boost the performance of your people and, hence, also of the organization. It will also help you to foster more cordial relationships, not only with your peers, but also with friends, spouse and family, and professionals in the outside world.

The book is a result of my deep interest and experience in mentoring and developing people, and its growing significance as sustainable competitive advantage.

It provides a number of sure-fire formulae to help managers to:

- inspire subordinates/team(s) to perform better through routine interactions,
- mentor/groom people effectively,
- provide post-appraisal counselling, i.e. communicating without demotivating, and
- establish mutually supportive and trusting relations with subordinates/colleagues/professional associates.

The strategies and approaches discussed here are relevant for managers at all levels, whether in a government or private organization and irrespective of its size. The book, therefore, can help you inspire and mentor people in both, the personal and professional space.

Conceptually, the book or the subject of changing, mentoring and developing, has been divided into two parts.

PART I:

One cannot mentor or develop people unless one evokes their trust and confidence. The first part of the book focuses on developing genuine and trustworthy relationships. Such a relationship, though not so easy to establish, is a foundation, a pre-requisite, without which mentoring cannot be effective.

PART II:

This part of the book focuses on hands-on practical strategies for leading and mentoring that may be applied in routine interactions.

Once trusting relationships are developed, people can be inspired and mentored to achieve better performance and behaviour.

The strategies for leading and mentoring, given in this book, promise to produce enhanced performance and trusting relationships when applied in everyday interactions. They are based on my observation of some renowned chief executive officers during my long innings as a consultant, my research when I was a faculty member at a leading business school, and as a trained psychotherapist, which ensured that suggested techniques are in conformity with the scientific knowledge of human behaviour and motivation. These resources have provided the rationale for suggesting these strategies, some of which convincingly suggest the replacement of a few popular prevalent beliefs and practices.

The objective of the book, therefore, is to make leaders more effective, transform managers into leaders and, on the personal front, become happier spouses, parents, friends and colleagues.

PART I

CREATING A FOUNDATION: IMPERATIVES
FOR SUCCESSFUL LEADING AND MENTORING

1

Mentoring and Developing
is Managing Change

ESSENCE AND ESSENTIALS OF INSPIRING, MENTORING AND PEOPLE DEVELOPMENT

Mentoring and developing people is not an altruistic activity. It is essential for any progressive organization, as well as in the interest of superiors, to enhance their own performance and position in the organization, with the help of people reporting to them. The success of managers depends to a great extent on how far they succeed in making their own people successful.

The need and importance of people development and mentoring, therefore, is not a moot issue, but the strategies and approaches to achieve the best results have stimulated the minds of many management practitioners and psychologists. The approaches, techniques and strategies discussed here are likely to produce highly positive results when put to practice.

MENTORING IS ADMINISTERING CHANGE

To understand and use the approaches and strategies of developing people, it is essential to first realize that mentoring or developing is a way of bringing about a *change* in people. For what else is development, but changing for the better or increasing one's motivation and improving one's habits (personal and professional), attitudes, skills, knowledge and concepts, and to apply them appropriately?

This has important implications. It implies that all the rules, mechanisms or strategies of managing a (personal) change become relevant while mentoring and developing human resource. It also means that every successful manager and, in fact, anyone desiring to bring a change in the behaviour, attitude or perception of a spouse, kith and kin, friend or a colleague, must necessarily become an effective 'change agent', i.e. a person with psychological insight into the dynamics of resistance to change and how to deal with it, though he/she need not necessarily be a psychologist.

HOW AND WHERE TO BEGIN?

To develop is to change. But will it happen if, with the best of intentions and in a mild manner, the boss was to tell someone, 'Please meet me this evening. I want to speak to you. I think you need to change…?'

You got it! The reaction is obvious. The brief interaction would have made the person feel uncomfortable the whole day. Here is what he might say to his colleagues: 'I have been here for so many years... No one ever asked me to change.

God knows why he wants me to change *now*! What does he think? What is wrong with me?'

The colleagues may also anxiously speculate; they might anticipate that they are next in queue; anxiety might grip everyone in the department!

When you tell someone—subordinate, friend or domestic help—that he/she is not good at his/her work, or not quite intelligent/honest/straightforward, even if you do so with the best of intentions, what is the response likely to be? Have you come across a person who would say, 'Yes, I agree with you; what you are saying is right.'?

This indicates that a suggestion to change or develop is, quite often, resisted. Before going into why change is resisted and how to overcome this sort of resistance, we have to answer these questions: Is change always resisted? Are all kinds of change resisted?

Not necessarily. If we are asked to move to a bigger, more luxurious home or office, or to a more prestigious or glamorous position, or to enjoy a multi-cuisine buffet instead of a simple meal, we offer no resistance to any of these suggestions. This is because we know that these changes do not affect us in an adverse manner; they do not cause us pain or agony. However, being summoned by a superior implies some sort of inadequacy, and accepting that one is not as good as one always thought oneself to be is painful as it hurts one's self-image. Further to the interaction, implementing the changes suggested by the superior may be even more daunting.

Not surprising then:

> *People do not mind change;*
> *they mind being changed.*

This means that change is not resisted unless it inflicts pain/agony on oneself. One does not mind taking charge of changing others as it inflicts no suffering to oneself. For precisely the same reason:

Everyone wants to change the world;
no one wants to change himself.

That apart, we do not always react in the same way to criticism or to suggestion(s) to change ourselves. Our reaction to such suggestions/criticism depends on various factors, which include:

- who is criticizing/suggesting a change i.e. our relationship with the person or our perception of him/her;
- what is being said;
- how harshly or mildly it is being said; and
- when or at what time; etc.

If the negative feedback about performance, behaviour and intention comes from someone whom we respect, trust and know as our well-wisher, it is better received. If it comes from a person who we know only formally or whose credentials as a well-wisher are not yet established, the feedback is resisted, though not always overtly. Hence, the mentor should first seek to establish trust. The comparison of two situations—on one hand, the suggestion to change coming from a trusted and well-respected person and, on the other hand, it coming from a person whose credentials are still shaky or unproven—do establish one *essential* condition that determines the success in developing and mentoring.

Mentoring, developing and, thus, changing people, is not possible unless they perceive their mentor (or anyone assuming that role) as genuinely interested in their development and their relationship is perceived as genuine and trustworthy.

A trustworthy relationship is a pre-requisite not only for a superior in an organization to develop his subordinates, but also to seek help and cooperation from his colleagues at a *lateral level* to achieve his and the organization's goals. Trust as the basis of relationship is highly important for bringing about change in the behaviour of a spouse, a teenage child, a friend, even a domestic help. A careful study of the rules and principles of creating mutual trust will greatly facilitate the development of harmonious and productive relations with all those you interact with in everyday life.

*People do not mind change, they
mind being changed!*

*This means that change is not resisted unless it
inflicts pain to oneself. For precisely the same reason,
no one minds taking charge for changing others, if
asked, as it inflicts no pain to oneself. Which is why:*

*Everyone wants to change the world; no one wants
to change himself...*

2

Developing Trust in Relationships:
A Pre-requisite for Mentoring

How PEOPLE resist/react when asked to change depends a lot on how the message is communicated. Try telling your spouse that he/she is in the habit of lying, nagging, or too slow to understanding things. You would like to see your spouse more capable and effective, therefore, you expect him/her to reveal the reasons/motivation behind present deficit or inadequacy in behaviour. However, the response or what your spouse will **overtly** say, which will invariably betray your expectations, is really meant to cover up the **covert** or *real* truth behind the manifest behaviour. It would either be a flat denial: 'You are totally wrong', or a retaliation: 'You always have been biased against me' or 'Have you seen yourself, your own defects?, or blaming the situation: 'I have been so stressed these days', or a justification: 'I have been doing it for your own/our good', and (other overt responses) so on...

If a superior tells his subordinate: 'The report that you have submitted is not up to my expectations' or 'You have taken too much time; you were to give me that much earlier...'

Though the intention of the superior is to help the subordinate to improve his/her performance, first, by identifying the problem areas so as to ensure that mistakes are not repeated or deficit performance is not recorded, he would fail to succeed by making such statements as they are likely to evoke resistance of subordinates since they are expected to admit their faults.

If they do what you (superior) expect, it would bring out the truth which normally remains at the covert level, and bring out the latent reality at the overt or manifest level.

But, invariably, what you will get are *overt* responses that hide the *covert* or real truth, like: 'The data was lacking', 'I did not get the information required to generate the report in time', 'Another senior gave me an assignment that had to be completed urgently', 'My junior let me down', or 'I had little help as my junior was on leave', and so on...

Now, as long as the subordinate continues to give excuses, development/improvement is not possible. Because as you react to what he says (which you know is fiction), he will come up with more excuses or hide the reality, and meaningless arguments will ensue, without any gains, change in behaviour or development.

To understand why criticism genuinely intended to help or achieve better performance is not accepted, we must understand why well-intended suggestions or genuine offers to change for better are resisted.

OVERCOMING RESISTANCE TO CHANGE

Attempts to develop or mentor can't succeed unless we understand why people resist it when it can actually help them improve.

Any suggestion to change is resisted, if:

- it involves uncertainty about the outcome (consequences) or one's capabilities of going through the processes involved in the change.
- it is threatening to one's self-image, i.e. not in agreement with one's self-image and self-esteem.

If one is assigned a task that one has never done before, it could create the fear of uncertainty about its outcome. If one is asked to learn a new skill in order to complete the task, it could instil the fear of failing to learn it. Such changes are likely to be resisted so as to avoid going through the discomfort of possible failure.

Let us go to the second and more common reason of why change is resisted. I have, earlier, merely given examples of how criticism is resisted with denials, blaming situations, etc., to cover inadequacy in behaviour and performance. Here is why.

We all believe that we are intelligent, morally upright, and have various positive attributes. We all have certain positive self-images. But these criticisms pointing out our various inadequacies, threaten or contradict our self-images. Their acceptance will weaken and create doubts of our self-identity or what we have believed ourselves to be, or hurt our ego. Such criticisms are best not entertained. Yet in the face of failings or inadequacies displayed, we are compelled to provide some explanation, though spurious, but believed to be true, so that we retain the status quo and continue living without doubts and anxieties.

This also means that if a suggested change does not hurt the self-image or create uncertainties, it may not be resisted or rejected. Offer someone to move to a bigger or better house or office, or to avail a discount coupon, no one will object. This is why I had said earlier: People don't mind change, they mind being changed, and everyone wants to change the world, but no one wants to change oneself.

- However, when our deficiencies are pointed out, we provide plausible explanations that appear rational and reasonable to the world and to ourselves. This enables us to cover up the reality and let it remain at the covert level, since its surfacing at the conscious level could cause dissonance or a crisis of identity. And this brings out the difference between what could be called '**manifest**' and '**latent**'.

Never forget that often there is a difference in what people say (manifest level) and what they mean (latent level).

- At the **latent level,** lies the real or hidden meaning of what is said overtly, and its overt acceptance could cause discomfort or psychological disturbance in a person.

- At the **manifest level**, people say things that look reasonable and rational, in order to disguise or cover up what lies at the latent level, so as to protect themselves from anxiety or discomfort.

That which is said to cover the real is called a defense

mechanism. Here are a few examples of various types of defense mechanisms.

Rationalization: I had no help or information.

Denial: You never told me you wanted it now.

Regression: I was not well.

Projections: Counter-attack, for instance, you always blame only me, etc.

Of course, there are many other types of defense mechanisms. The purpose is to explain the undercurrents of communication and why a mentor has to look beyond what is said to deal with defense mechanisms effectively.

THE CHALLENGE OF DEALING WITH DEFENSES

To inspire and mentor people, you have to help them to recognize and accept their flaws, and thus, bring the latent to the manifest level.

The challenge for a mentor is to break the defense mechanisms in a way that they are not required anymore. In other words, the people, whom you want to help to change/ develop, should not feel discomfort in accepting their flaws, which would have otherwise hurt their self-esteem or sense of security.

Here are the three **principles** which a mentor or developer could deploy to deal with defenses and create trusting relationships.

THREE PRIME PRINCIPLES OF DISSOLVING DEFENSES AND DEVELOPING MUTUAL TRUST

Principle 1: Never Be Judgemental

Since defense mechanisms, or 'latent' as distinct from 'manifest', exist to protect an individual from anxiety and loss of self-esteem, a mentee must feel assured that by confessing or bringing out the latent, he will not be condemned, judged or evaluated negatively by his mentor/superior/counsellor. If you become judgemental or start blaming him when he is making an effort to change by trying to transform the latent into the manifest, he will further strengthen his defenses in the future. No matter how well-intended and mildly conveyed, fault-finding and criticism will result in his shutting up and restricting healthy communication. This may also result in you, the superior, creating a chasm and hostilities between the two of you.

The role of a mentor is to encourage an individual to realize and admit his inadequacies, without fear and anxiety, thereby creating genuine, trustworthy relationships.

Should a mentor give advice at all?

The answer to that is 'No'! Superiors probably have more experience, are likely to be wiser, have gone through such situations, seen it all and done it, as they say. Yet it is not the role of a mentor to advice and keep suggesting what to do.

The role of a superior, leader or mentor is to *develop* his people. Telling him what to do or what not to do, or what is right or wrong, does not in any way lead to development. Giving expert advice or opinion is the job of a 'consultant' or even a 'guide'. There is difference between a consultant and a mentor. The distinction between a consultant and a mentor needs to be clearly understood. A consultant provides expert advice, while a mentor helps develop expertise or competencies to think independently, generate various alternatives, evolve criteria for evaluation and select the best options under the circumstances. A consultant uses his expertise and recommends options that one may pursue to reach his/her goal, while a mentor helps one to develop one's expertise to think and take one's own decisions. The mentor helps develop these 'inner' resources instead of providing the mentee his expert counsel. That is what leads to development: developing capabilities to take independent decisions instead of being habitually dependent on the superior for taking all sorts of decision or advice. This holds good in personal life and in the organizational setting, too, where the manager must make his subordinates capable of replacing him. The responsibility of a mentor is to be the 'enabler' and not a 'disabler' who cannot think or decide without him.

Finally, there are major individual differences amongst people: the mentor isn't you, just as you are not him. Probably the outcome that would please him is not the same that pleases you, as his aspirations and likes and dislikes are different. Also, what is achievable by you and him is not the same, as the skills and knowledge which you both have vary widely. These differences account for individual identities. As this has been discussed again at the end of book, let me briefly express the position here that the mentor is not supposed to try and change the identity of a mentee. Instead, respecting his individuality, he should let him take decisions which would fulfil his unique

The challenge for a mentor or developer is to stop the operations of defense mechanisms in such a way that they are no more required. In other words, the people you want to change or develop should not feel discomfort or pain in accepting the realities which normally hurt their self-esteem or sense of security that activate defenses.

needs, aspirations and interests. This reasoning is compatible with the earlier one of not being judgemental, because that not only results in silencing him for fear of negative evaluation, but is made in context of the needs and the value system of the mentor, not the mentee.

Principle 2: Exude Warmth and Optimism

The reception of feedback also depends on who is offering it. No one can motivate, inspire, mentor or develop subordinates, or bring about change in a colleague, friend or a family member without a genuine desire for their well-being. It is, therefore, essential that a mentor exudes warmth and connects with the mentees so that they are on the same emotional plane. A superior should be seen as sympathetic, appreciative and genuinely interested in understanding the problems of the person whom he intends to help.

Apart from warmth, it is also essential that a mentor conveys hope and optimism to a mentee that he is capable of successfully carrying out the intended change and bringing it to fruition. If a mentor does not convey it, the mentee might remain sceptical, unlikely to feel enthusiastic and may not put in his best efforts to complete the task successfully.

However, the mentor should also ensure that the mentee does not get so emotionally involved that he loses the objectivity required for executing the task assigned to him. In this respect, a mentor is like an able surgeon who is genuinely concerned about his patients but does not get emotionally over-involved as that could prove counter-productive. The thumb rule is to exude sympathy and optimism without getting emotionally too involved.

Principle 3: Be Congruent

Congruence is very important. If a mentor does not practise congruence, he will not succeed in establishing relationships that may help people improve. An extreme example of incongruence would be a drunken person, who after losing control over his walk and talk, proclaims that he is not drunk or that alcohol had no effect on him. Congruence is consistency between what one is really feeling and thinking, being aware of it, and what one says or communicates. However, what some people say is a farce; one may not know what they really mean, and one is always cautious in dealing with them.

Some people manage to lie with a straight face. Those who are not congruent may think that they can manage to get away with their lack of transparency and others cannot make out that they don't mean what they say. The fact is that, in most cases, people can intuitively see the duplicity or lack of transparency in behaviour. Even if they are not sure, they somehow 'feel' uneasy or uncomfortable with such people. Obviously, lack of transparency creates barriers in communication; the person you intend to help does not perceive you as a well-wisher. Your claim to the contrary notwithstanding, he starts indulging in defensive behaviour.

It is important to emphasize the fact that congruence is required in what one is thinking and feeling internally and what one says overtly. Congruence is consistency between what one is really feeling and thinking, being aware of it, and what one says or communicates. What one says, one's facial expressions and body language should also be in congruence. If you are narrating a bad experience…and after listening to your story, someone tells you that he is feeling sad about what happened, but at the same time he is looking elsewhere, scribbling in his diary or yawning, you know not to trust what he is saying.

Congruence is essential to establish credibility. One can relate to some individuals easily because one knows that they mean and are sincere about what they say; they are aware of what they think and feel. Congruence or total transparency is essential for the growth and enhancement of trust in a relationship. The greater the congruence in what a mentor says and means, the lesser the barriers in communication and hence, they would share a more positive relationship.

Congruence is consistency between what one is really feeling and thinking, being aware of it, and what one says or communicates. It is essential for establishing credibility.

One can relate to some individuals easily because one knows that they are sincere and they mean what they say, and they are aware about what they think and feel. Once their credibility is established, one knows how to relate to them. However, what some people say is a farce; one may not know what they really mean, and one is always cautious in dealing with them.

TO SUMMARIZE

To help develop your people, you must evolve the relationship and take it beyond the protective defenses we all deploy regularly. These defenses are deployed to protect the self-image and self-esteem of people which is threatened by the criticism of inadequacies, even when intended to bring about improvement in them. To break these defenses, it is important to create an environment of acceptance. Such an environment is created by empathy, optimism, encouragement to open up by being non-judgemental and being authentic in communicating, i.e. ensuring what one communicates, verbally or through gestures, is congruent with what one genuinely feels or believes. Before discussing how we practise these principles to get the desired results, it is important to recall another essential condition we stipulated for developing trust: you cannot mistrust a person and expect him to trust you, for only trust begets trust.

PRACTISING THE THREE PRINCIPLES

How do we put these principles into practice (being non-judgemental, empathetic and congruent), so that those whose behaviour you seek to change, willingly accept you as their mentor? Whatever the principles, ultimately, your effectiveness as a change agent and developer of your people depends upon your communication, i.e. what and how you communicate.

To practise these principles, keep in mind these 'Dos and Don'ts' of communication for nurturing *any* relationship—be it that with a spouse, friend or colleague, but especially for developing people who are capable of performing better.

DON'TS

Never use these statements when you assume the role of a mentor.

Please repeat: This shows that you are not listening; also, it is not easy to repeat emotionally-heavy matter. If you have not fully understood, say 'I think what you were saying is important, though I am not sure that I have fully understood it...' and the likes. He should not feel that you were not attentive.

I do not understand you: With this, he knows he wasted his time. He should not feel that you are also like others who do not understand him.

I don't agree with you. You are not correct here: This shows that you are being judgemental. He will recall the 'same old story'; you are no different.

I fully/totally agree with you: No one could be so sure. Even he might find it difficult or too good to believe.

I don't think this point/issue is important: This will communicate that you are not empathetic/understanding. This issue may not be important for you, but for him, it is.

Let us talk of something else: This may convey that you are not sensitive towards his concerns. He has to decide what is important or what is troubling him. Don't forget, you are meeting for his sake.

I don't think you have understood my point: Oh, my! You, as a mentor, have to understand him. The purpose of meeting is that you understand him; not the other way round.

DOS

Make sure you follow these rules when mentoring.

Observe and pay full attention: Listening is more than passive hearing; it involves observing and paying attention. Don't fall for the temptation to interrupt and say, 'I know what you want to say. I have gone though that myself...' You might have gone through it, but he is probably feeling differently. Observe not only what the person is saying, but also his gestures, feelings, etc. Learn to read body language, if possible.

Say 'yes' often: Communicate that you are hearing by nodding occasionally.

Re-phrase and summarize: Saying the same thing in different words would help you both to resolve any ambiguity and ensure that you are on the same page.

Encourage: A mentor should encourage the mentee to express his thoughts by saying, 'Tell me a little more' or 'Let me understand this little better.

Empathize/sympathize: A mentor should try to empathize with the mentee by saying something like, 'I know how you are feeling...'

Mind your body language: If you are genuinely interested, your gestures, facial expressions, tone and choice of words etc., should convey the same thing that your words do.

These 'Dos and Don'ts' will help a great deal in executing or putting in practice the three principles of communication which are aimed at breaking the defenses and creating mutually-trusting relationships, the first of the two conditions for transforming people. Initially, you may have to make a conscious effort, but you would soon be practising them as a matter of habit.

DEMONSTRATING YOUR TRUST RECIPROCITY: THE FOUNDATION FOR BUILDING TRUST

Trust by definition is reciprocal in nature. It is mutual: trust begets trust. If you trust someone, he too will trust you. You are unlikely to trust someone who does not trust you. The relationship in which one person does not trust the other either ceases to exist or is transformed into a mutually-trusting relationship over the course of time.

It is not enough to trust a person. It is important to convey it convincingly. But how to demonstrate it in a manner that the other person also reciprocates in the same measure?

First, tell him in a matter-of-fact manner that in your opinion, he is intelligent, a good human being, or a man of principles, or whatever is appropriate, and that you appreciate him for those qualities. Taking it further, when the occasion arises, seek his help or ask for a favour, telling him that you are requesting him because you trust and depend more on him than anyone else around. Chances are that not only will he help you if he can, but it will also establish a mutually-trusting bond between you two.

You could even translate your words into action and

demonstrate your trust in him if he is your reportee in the organization. Should you find him worthy of it, empower him with some special assignment that could earn him some recognition and tell him that in your opinion, you could trust him to do justice to that important assignment. This will not only earn you his gratitude, but trust in you for the long time to come.

EMPATHY GENERATES TRUST

One can become a great leader, capable of inspiring, motivating and taking people to the next level, if and only if one can empathize.

Empathy is getting into the shoes of other people, to see and feel the world as they do. It provides a framework within which the strategies and techniques discussed in this book would work; outside the framework or when practised in the absence of empathy, most of them will fall flat or prove ineffective.

Why is empathy so crucial in determining the effectiveness of strategies?

Mentoring and developing people involves changing the way they feel, perceive, behave, aspire, etc. Now, how could one change these dynamics, unless one knows how people at the moment are 'seeing', 'perceiving', 'aspiring', etc., or without wearing the spectacles they are wearing? Can one appreciate what another person is feeling without feeling the same way oneself? Yes; and that's what is meant by empathy and it is essential for developing, mentoring and changing people. Therefore, if it's not in one to empathize, one might not be able to successfully deploy these strategies to develop people.

ESTABLISHING 'RAPPORT', 'EQUATION' AND 'WAVELENGTH'

Empathy is crucially important in an organizational setting. However, its exceedingly crucial role in nurturing and sustaining healthy relationships among spouses, friends etc., is either grossly underestimated or not understood. We keep talking about the importance of '*developing an equation*', '*being on a same wavelength*', and '*establishing a rapport*' in the context of social and business relations. How is all this achieved? Of course, through right communication. It would be interesting and useful to understand the nature and dynamics of this communication, which leads to a great rapport or similar wavelenghts. I said earlier that empathy stems from the 'emotional connect', i.e. when one person experiences or re-lives the perceptions, feelings and aspirations of others. In other words, one shares something that is in the realm of experiences of the other person. When communication begins or takes off with something that is in the realm of experience of others, we develop a mutual understanding, rapport, equation, or are on the same wavelength. Communication, which is aimed at mentoring people or sustaining or reinforcing relationships, should contain the experiences that are part of the repertoire of experiences of the other person. Communication which is not the part of repertoire of experiences of the other person is not likely to prove effective, or much understood, as it creates a 'communication gap'.

To sum it, the much-valued *rapport, equation* and *wavelength* are euphemisms or expressions of empathy. They all connote empathy and are achieved first by connecting with the 'inner world' of a person's feelings, attitudes and perceptions, and then ensuring that common or shared experiences become the starting point of communication.

A leader has to be humble and learn a great deal from 'followers'. One cannot empathize unless one forgets about one's own self and focuses on learning about the world of followers to become an effective 'change agent'. For the proud egoist, this often means 'climbing down' to the level of 'followers'. But unless he is willing to get into the shoes of 'lesser' ones, and 'learn' about them and the world they live in, he is unlikely to succeed as a leader. The leaders and those aspiring to lead, instead of living in their ivory towers, must, therefore, inculcate within them the virtue of humility and learn a great deal from followers. This is what Martin Luther King had in mind when he said, *'Everyone can be great because anyone can serve.'*

Inspiring, mentoring and developing people, therefore, is indeed a tough task for those who are **insensitive** and cannot empathize. Only those who are genuinely interested in their people can empathize and sustain it over a long period of time. This puts natural limitations on those who aspire for the role of a leader, mentor or change agent. It also explains why some people cannot be good mentors, developers or leaders (and answers the question whether everybody could be trained to be a leader). On the other hand, if one is naturally sensitive and interested in understanding people, the practices and strategies suggested in the following pages would surely help one discover a leader within oneself, who could energize and inspire people to produce better results.

Having emphasized the importance of empathy for a leader, we now move on to the practical strategies which a leader could deploy in day-to-day interactions. But before that, let us make a bridge between establishing the emotional connect, which we have learnt and discussed so far, and the techniques and strategies for developing and mentoring people.

The much-valued rapport, equation and wavelength are euphemisms or expressions of empathy. They all connote empathy and are achieved first by connecting with the 'inner world' of a person's feelings, attitudes and perceptions, and then ensuring that common or shared experiences become the starting point of communication.

PRELUDE TO PART II

FROM EMOTIONS TO ABILITY;
FROM TRUST TO TECHNIQUE

We have so far focused on the fact that relationships based on trust and emotional connect are essential for mentoring, developing and changing people. This, however, is never enough to change or mentor people. A good teacher, after inspiring and motivating his students, must impart knowledge or skills to develop them. Trust and relationships are the emotive aspects of the development; they create the platform or conditions for using the ability, strategy and/or techniques required in the development process. The human personality can be classified in two components: the emotive world (motivations and emotions) and the capabilities (abilities or intelligence component). The success of any human endeavour depends on adequately deploying both of them. And the success of the mentor or change agent, once he has created the emotive bond, will depend on his ability or social intelligence, and are reflected in the strategies a mentor deploys in: what he says, to whom, when, how, while reprimanding, criticizing, rewarding and delegating, etc.

TO SUMMARIZE

Inspiring, developing and mentoring is not possible without creating trust and using techniques or strategies for development. Trust is built on emotive bonds; modifying someone's behaviour (development) depends further on the ability to deploy social intelligence or practical techniques and skills, after successfully establishing trust. In order to mentor people, either in their personal or professional lives, one needs to know what one wants to communicate and decide on the most appropriate strategy of what and how to say it, to obtain the desired behaviour. Part II of the book outlines a number of techniques or practical strategies for deploying them in day-to-day interactions.

PART II

PRACTICAL DAY-TO-DAY STRATEGIES
FOR INSPIRING AND MENTORING PEOPLE
FOR PEAK PERFORMANCE

1

Strategies and Techniques for Evoking the Desired Response

ASK SIMPLE QUESTIONS

To begin with, here is the simplest technique of all, because simple techniques are often more effective than complex ones. Having served as a consultant for long to a widely known multinational company, I had observed that a very renowned CEO had the habit of stopping by one of the executives, whoever caught his attention, just before he left office in the evening, or at times before lunch. He would sit and chat with him informally and amicably for about 10 minutes. One day, when I asked what he was up to, he said that this was one of his ways to keep in touch with his people, know their problems and try to help if he could, so that they felt cared for and charged to deliver their best.

Now, forget the complex motivational theories taught at

business schools. Just go over and ask your subordinates simple questions. Do not stand over their heads or stop by when you are in a hurry; sit down to speak to them leisurely for a few minutes. Ask them: 'Tell me how your work is progressing?', 'How are you doing?' or 'How are things with you?'. You would be surprised that in most cases they would tell you some 'petty' things that have become major irritants in their performance, for instance, a seating arrangement that has robbed them of their privacy, a temporary shortage of cash or something regarding the organization which you should know about, an increase in work-load, uncertainty of future prospects, etc. You would be amazed at the way the CEO removed many 'petty' irritants that had become major barriers to their motivation to perform better.

What the CEO achieved through this practice, is extremely important. By spending about 10 minutes a day with a member of his staff, he maintained close contact with his people, effectively conveyed his concern for them, developed a rapport, and often removed major 'petty' irritants; his simple act included all the elements of inspiring, motivating and developing people.

Leading and motivating is important, but that does not mean we make it complicated and esoteric. This cannot be used as a gimmick or foolery, because people can see through the pretensions, which will boomerang and damage relations. But if practised genuinely, you would realize that these are probably the most productive 10 minutes you spend to keep people charged and get the best results.

FOCUS ON STRENGTHS, NOT ON
ELIMINATING WEAKNESSES

How often have you heard that a good manager coaches or helps his people overcome their weaknesses to make them more effective? To realize how dumb a thing it is to say, just think for how long you have been trying to change your spouse, sibling, friend and child, and where do you stand now with all your efforts all these years. Removing weaknesses may require all the time and effort on earth, which you cannot spare, and you might end up feeling frustrated. Even a professional psychologist or therapist may take years to help people to change and yet end up nowhere. The primary job of a manager is not to help people overcome their weaknesses; it is to coach them to acquire new skills and knowledge. Even if you do succeed by some miraculous efforts to shed the unproductive past patterns of your subordinates, you would still achieve nothing unless you train them to deploy the strengths and abilities to perform the tasks they have been assigned.

Organizational effectiveness and the genius of the manager lies in delegating the tasks to people based on their strengths.

Should a superior help his subordinates overcome their weaknesses, which significantly affect their performance?

An effective leader does so without making any extra effort. Instead of spending his time tutoring or counselling his subordinates, he may give them the responsibility for projects that call for skills/knowledge that they lack. He should give them a bit more time, and tell them that while they could consult him, he expects them to do a good job. This would help them to learn what they are doing incorrectly and improve upon the same on their own. Lessons which are learnt from 'learning by doing' actually last much longer than a leader telling people what to do and what not to do.

Let us assume you have an Area Sales Manager who sends widely off-the-mark demand forecasts to Operations Department, which uses it for purchasing material. Tell him that this has become a major problem and that you have decided to give him this assignment to solve the problem of bad forecasting. This will prompt him to learn and overcome his deficiencies. Here, you have given him the chance to identify the issues, fix them, and take pride in coming out as a winner. Take the example of a sales executive who frequently goes missing from the field. Tell him that you have decided to give him the responsibility of keeping a check on the sales force, so that instances of goofing around come down drastically. Chances are that his own goofing bouts of truancy will cease and he may find out a brilliant way to keep a check on the same!

The important principle involved here is: if your subordinate has a major inadequacy which is coming in the way of his performance, make sure that he takes the responsibility of overcoming it himself, re-learning preferably by doing, rather than you sermoning or tutoring him.

Let us keep in mind that the objective of development is to move from doing just those things that one has always been doing, to doing new things or doing things in new ways, thereby adding new skills/knowledge to the existing repartee.

It is, therefore, undoubtedly wiser to concentrate on identifying, building and riding on the strengths of people, though it is prudent to not remain ignorant of their weaknesses.

DO NOT IGNORE THE LESSON THAT DIFFERENTIATES SUCCESS FROM FAILURE

Often, what differentiates successful organizations from others is that the latter do not work on priorities, act on wrong priorities, or are unable to implement strategies to get the priority tasks done. This, however, is even truer of what differentiates the effective and non-effective executives. This is like forgetting the fact that tomorrow arrives only for those who take care of surviving today. A superior must be clear about the priorities at hand. Having done so, he cannot fail to communicate and assign the priority tasks to his subordinates. If the senior fails to do this, he cannot hold the subordinates responsible for unsatisfactory results. This is not an uncommon scenario in organizations, when priority tasks remain unattended to, as their urgency and importance has not been communicated to subordinates in time. Some individuals may lack the capability of differentiating the woods from trees. It's, therefore, up to the boss to spell out the priorities.

At times, seniors do get infuriated when they find that important tasks have not been accomplished in the given time, in spite of having communicated their significance and priority. There could be many reasons for this, apart from those already mentioned. Some of us have a tendency to postpone certain tasks either because they are a bit too difficult and involve hardwork (many of us wish to first do the simpler tasks that involve little effort) or because we postpone a task we dislike or find disinteresting. Though it is not the job of a superior to attempt to modify this behaviour, it is essential that he ensures that his people learn to focus on high-priority tasks consistently. The organizational setting may also be used to tell subordinates that if they do not work on the basis of priorities, their contribution and their role in the organization may be marginalized.

Setting priorities and acting on them is essential not only in an organization, but also in our personal lives—a far more complex, involving and difficult process. However, setting the priorities correctly and acting in accordance to them is what determines the outcome, whether in an organization or in life.

MAKE IT PARTICIPATIVE: PARTICIPATION HAS MORE BENEFITS THAN YOU CAN IMAGINE

Participation is the most powerful tool, not only for developing people, but also for organizational and self-development. Though much talked about since long, many of its benefits as a development tool have still been grossly underestimated. It has unlimited potential to do good: to subordinates, to seniors who practise it, and for organizations. Determine not only the goals and strategies jointly with the subordinates, but involve them also in planning activities, schedules and resolution of problems as they arise. Here are some of the exceptional benefits of this simple-to-practise tool.

First, its obvious benefit is that subordinates get to learn a lot from it. And if the participation includes being part of different task groups and committees, it broadens the horizons and becomes an excellent tool for grooming executives for senior positions or positions demanding a wider perspective.

Second, since no one is an island in oneself, it becomes a very good device for learning even for the superior who presides over the group. Let us remember that creativity is no one's monopoly. Even a worker can at times come up with an idea worth a million dollars. It is, therefore, wise if the organization makes the best use of all its human resources using the participative technique.

Third, the interactive process in a group has the potential of developing more innovative ideas, and new approaches for solutions of the problems, which the superior might not have thought of on his own.

Fourth, participating in a group gives a sense of pride and enhances self-esteem of the participating individuals, which enhances their motivation to bring out their best.

Fifth, the quality of decision-making improves, because the subordinates might talk about some practical problems that arise at the grass-roots level while implementing the plans, which the superior might not be aware of, and offer some practical solutions.

Sixth, and probably most importantly, since decisions are taken jointly instead of individually by a superior, they are more likely to carry personal commitment of the participating individuals. When one endorses anything as a group, we tend to live by it. Motivationally, it is much easier to make an all-out effort for the results one is personally committed to, as compared to making efforts for the results imposed by others. And that makes all the difference!

Lastly, and the corollary of the above, there would most likely be some members who are not fully convinced of the group's decision. If it is essential to ensure the unflinching commitment of all participants, it would be much better to make minutes of the meeting soon enough, get the signature of all participants and circulate the minutes among the concerned corporate members. And in important or appropriate cases, it would be even better if they are personally announced to a larger concerned audience in the presence of all the participants of the group. The suggestion is based on a psychological principle that members tend to support the stand they have taken *publicly* even if not convinced fully initially. It is, therefore, desirable to announce the group's decisions publicly (i.e. among wider and relevant audience) with the endorsement of all participating members.

Practise participation profusely, from the board to the shop-floor level, not only to inspire and develop your people and for better execution but also for personal growth and enhancing organizational performance.

TASK-ORIENTATION MUST SUPERSEDE CONCERN FOR PEOPLE

An issue which is palpably oldest and is constantly being discussed since the dawn of the industrial revolution has come to be known as people- vs task-orientation. In spite of it, the lack of clarity continues. There has been an over-simplification in describing effective leadership style on this parameter. Even the perennial question 'Should a leader be people-oriented or task-focused?', based on this typology of people- vs work-orientation still remains to be satisfactorily answered.

My own reflections and the research that I did during my tenure as faculty at a prominent business school (IIMA)

Motivationally, it is much easier to make an all-out effort for the results one is personally committed to, as compared to making efforts for the results imposed by others.

which was later published (*Psychological Report*, USA) and my experience as a consultant thereafter, led to one clear conclusion. While task-orientation is essential in every organization and in every situation, the role and importance of people-orientation varies widely from one situation to another.

How the relative role of people-orientation varies from one type of organization to the other is clearly brought about by just one example. I have often talked about the distinction between 'Achievement' and 'Affiliative' systems. The family as a primary affiliative system survives only as long as emotional and affective bonds exist among members. In fact, the system breaks up when 'family heads' like the father or mother, introduce other parameters like achievement as a criterion for membership or status in the family.

A mother does not withhold affection from an underperforming or a physically or mentally challenged child, nor showers all her love on a high-achieving child. The family survives as long as there is love among the members. Now, let us look at a work organization, which is an 'Achievement' system. An organization survives on and only as long as it manages to achieve its objectives, whether it is profits or service to the society. It is an achievement system because it will survive only as long as it achieves its objectives and not as long as emotional bonds exist among its members. In an organization, therefore, primacy of task-orientation is absolutely mandatory. (Yet, many promoters-CEOs, especially of Indian family-run organizations, are often lauded for operating their organizations like an extended family. This apparently makes no sense). Let me add in the

While task-orientation is essential in every organization and in every situation, the role and importance of people-orientation varies widely from one situation to another.

same breath, that human considerations, of course, cannot be ignored because members of the organization are human beings. However, it is important not to overlook the fact that they have been organized for achieving a particular task. Giving primacy to people-orientation is to misconceive the very nature and purpose of the existence of an organization. While a superior should empathize and understand the emotional state of his subordinates so as to develop insight into the dynamics underlying their behaviour, it is recommended that he should not get 'involved' in any manner that would hamper or upset work relations.

The research that I did has to be reviewed against the background of the fact that so many who pioneered Human Relations movement, such as Chris Argyris, have advocated that human beings must be given opportunities to satisfy their need for independence, being responsible adults. My study was to understand this very nature of the 'need for dependence and independence' and the way it manifests in work organizations. Unexpectedly, but very unambiguously, the findings were that the need for dependence (or independence) was bi-dimensional or bi-polar, i.e. the need for 'work dependence', (shown, for instance, in seeking detailed instructions at work) was quite different from 'emotional dependence' (shown, in trying to get closer at a personal level, developing mutual liking, etc.) If work and emotional dependence are two different tendencies or needs, the implications of findings are far reaching. Apart from the implications for training, the findings imply that prescription for superiors cannot be as simplistic as providing freedom and latitude in work, as made out by Human Relationists. To inspire people in real life, the leadership style has to vary depending on the 'work' and 'emotional' needs of the people. Some people do not care much for people-orientation or emotional ties. While in other cases of large number of adults with emotional and affiliative needs, their superior, even by providing the freedom and independence at work, cannot abdicate his responsibility of ensuring that emotional needs of his subordinates are gratified. The responsibility of a leader is to help subordinates perform a task, an end in itself. In some cases, he could do that by being primarily task-oriented. In other cases, where subordinates are emotionally dependent, he (as a strategist) should help them gratify their needs as a means to obtain the performance or results he seeks. And in order to be able to differentiate between the two types of people, he needs to be sensitive and empathetic.

More importantly, the study shows that it is essential to replace 'task- vs people orientation' with 'meaningful work vs emotional relationships'. Instead of balancing people vs task suggestion of grid theorists (into 5:5 or 9:9), prudence demands that with greater understanding of dependence–independence needs (emotional and work dependence), now, the superior should vary his style or relationships with each subordinate based on the latter's individual needs for work and emotional dependence/independence.

And since task- or work-orientation is always important in Achievement system, his supervisory style should vary from say 5-1 to 5-9 based on a subordinate's emotional needs; or from 6-1 to 9-1 or 6-9, based on the subordinate's need for seeking detailed instructions and intensity of emotional needs. I am sure the experienced readers would know of many instances when performance suffered because of a superior's undersupervision and freedom, which he provided in work as recommended by an earlier misconstrued theory. And surely the readers have come across many subordinates who are quite happy with good 'working' relations, unconcerned about seeking closeness which they don't consider necessary. A superior would certainly benefit much more by tailoring his style on his understanding of work and emotional dependence needs of his subordinates, as clearly shown by my research cited earlier, (*Psychological Report*, USA, 1970 and *The Indian Journal of Industrial Relations*, 1970), instead of relying on the traditional 'task- vs people-orientation' typology.

The study shows that it is essential to replace 'task-vs people-orientation' with 'meaningful work vs emotional relationships'. Instead of balancing 'people vs task' suggestion of grid theorists (into 5:5 or 9:9), prudence demands that with greater understanding of dependence–independence needs (emotional and work dependence), now, the superior should vary his style or relationships with each subordinate based on the latter's individual needs for work and emotional dependence/independence.

2

Rewards and Punishment

Reward and punishment are probably the only two means or devices to mould or influence the behaviour of people. This is true at all ages, though the nature of rewards and punishments change as we grow.

A child grows into an adult through the process of learning, which involves regulation of his behaviour by his parents, who either reward (give a candy, cash, or a pat, when he behaves desirably) or punish (threat, rebuke, frighten or spank, to stop him from repeating wrongdoings) him. As he joins school, his learning and discipline continues through other means, and authorities ensure that he performs as well as he can in his behaviour and studies. These two most powerful instruments of regulating and developing behaviour continue to play their most powerful roles as he enters a work organization.

However, the means of delivering the two instruments of moulding behaviour become more subtle keeping in view our better-developed sensitivities and capabilities of learning as adults. In the ensuing discussion, the 'punishment' in context of organizations, therefore, implies giving negative feedback: criticism, like 'not up to the mark' or 'had expected better, reprimanding, or perhaps withholding increments. The rewards likewise include praising or commending someone's work, promotions or additional salary hikes. The examples indicate that rewards may take both forms: monetary and non-monetary incentives.

Rewards and punishments play an immensely important role in determining the morale and motivation of employees or executives at all the levels in an organization. But it is really painful to note that the two most powerful instruments or devices to influence or mould behaviour are most misused, because their dynamics and effects are least understood by managers, who use them regularly. Punishment, in particular, which has the potential of being used for developmental purposes, is very widely misused, resulting instead in demotivation and loss of morale of the managers who are punished. The training in use of these potent devices has been fully ignored. A misuse of punishment, as a result of ignorance in using it, is an epidemic, which is doing great damage to the motivation and development of people on whom we depend.

Here are few techniques and strategies that will, hopefully, help managers to make the right use of these highly potent devices, not only in corporate life, but also in transforming relationships with their spouses, friends and members of their family.

The discussion on punishment, somewhat more complex, will follow that on rewards.

REWARD LAVISHLY

Praise or any reward has been the greatest ever contrivance for motivating, learning and creating a positive bond. Some psychologists believe that learning is not possible, at all, without reward and reinforcement of what is to be learnt. (Here, reward has a wide connotation. It could be a promotion, pat, compliment, praise or a monetary reward). Praising or rewarding, whether in personal or work life, results in lot of benefits for all involved.

First of all, praise is a great morale booster: it improves self-esteem, confidence and determination to succeed.

The problem, however, is to identify the right occasions to praise or compliment a person. One obvious opportunity to do so is when one has done something good or right or completed a task satisfactorily. Second, a more powerful opportunity, though usually wasted, comes your way when you observe something positive in a person (his strength). Complimenting a person about his strength, be it his presentation, or written or persuasive skills, has something like a magical effect. Pleased with the positive feedback, especially by someone like one's superior, would make people want to inculcate that specific attribute for which they have been complimented as part of their self-image. A proven psychological truth is that people always want to live up to their self-images. If you happen to spot good attributes, telling them about it is the easiest way to bring in them long or enduring changes. They will live up to their new self-images.

Secondly, a number of experiments have shown, that rewards tremendously improve the probability of rewarded behaviour or high performance being repeated, whether the rewarded person is a child or a mature professional. Reward a gambler just a couple of times, and see him keep trying a lot more often. Compliment an executive for producing a good strategy or operation report and you immensely increase the chance of him doing a good job next time. So, do praise or pat people for good work, even if it is in pursuit of your own selfish ends! Lastly, but perhaps most importantly, praising your subordinates for good work strengthens your bond and improves the relationship between you two. Subordinates are willing to put in efforts for the one who appreciates them.

But how should one deliver reward for greater effectiveness?
Many people are stingy and believe that rewarding people often, will spoil them. They find it difficult to praise a person. The truth, however, is that being miserly with praise is counter-productive: such people are missing out the opportunity of using the greatest motivational device when it presents itself. Therefore, while you should not believe in that junk that too much praise will spoil a person, you surely don't have to exaggerate every petty achievement, for you will then lose the power of reward as an inspirational device. Researches have also proved that rewarding intermittently or randomly is as effective, if not more, than rewarding always or regularly. Rewarding often enough is, in fact, better than rewarding a person each and every time he performs well.

Research has also shown that the effect of reward or praise

is maximum when it is delivered immediately: it is practically none if delayed or postponed too long after it is due. Call your boys to pat them immediately after they have finished a task successfully. It makes no sense telling them that 'You know quite some time back or many months back, you had done that good work. I wanted to compliment you for that.' Be swift; don't wait for an ominous day.

To sum it, never miss out on the golden opportunity to praise genuine development, and lose no time to make use of the most powerful tool to inspire and develop people.

PUNISHING OR REPRIMANDING

How, when, how much to punish or reprimand for best results

Just as praise is a terrific morale booster, punishment is a terrible demotivator, with potential to inflict multiple damages to all involved—the giver as well as the receiver.

('Punishment', here refers to forms of punishment meted out to mature adults, like admonishing, being critical, expressing displeasure, or withholding increments in rare cases.) Spare the rod, spoil the child might be all right in books, but admonishing or criticizing your people can be useful only when done wisely and after understanding its inherent dangers, its limited scope and applicability, and, equally important, using all the skills of delivering it. The dynamics of how and when to reprimand are complex. Broadly, there are two major aspects that lead to its misuse: One, result of not understanding its limitations; second, lack of skills of reprimanding.

The discussion here is, therefore, divided in two parts:

- *limitations of reprimanding, or when to give negative feedback, criticize or admonish*; and
- *skills of reprimanding, or how to reprimand.*

LIMITATIONS ARISING FROM THE INHERENT INCAPABILITY OF A PERSON

Inadequacy in performance could result either from (a) negligence and lack of application, or (b) from inadequate knowledge, experience or skills required for the task. There are the two distinct reasons for the failure to perform well: negligence and incapability. But how many times does one analyse the real reason for the sub-standard performance before blasting out at the cook who has not prepared the dish to your expectations? (Was it due to his incapability and lack of experience in making it, in spite of the best intentions; or carelessness in spite of his capabilities perhaps proved earlier?) Or at your manager for the flaws in the project report resulting again either from negligence and indifference or from insufficient knowledge or experience in preparing such reports. If deficiencies or mistakes have not been caused by carelessness and indifference, but for inexperience or insufficient capabilities required for the job, it is like whipping the lame horse for not winning the race. Punishing the person for his incapacity to deliver is not only senseless, but also a poor reflection of a superior's capabilities of judging people before assigning them the task. It is your mistake, not his, to begin with. But punishing people for their indifferent attitude or negligence, when they

If deficiencies or mistakes have not been caused by carelessness and indifference, but for inexperience or insufficient capabilities required for the job, it is like whipping the lame horse for not winning the race. Punishing the person for his incapacity to deliver is not only senseless, but also a poor reflection of a superior's capabilities of judging people before assigning them the task. It is your mistake, not his, to begin with.

had the needed capabilities, is the right use of punishment. In fact, not punishing or reprimanding negligence is as bad as encouraging it. Not to discriminate between the two situations is the attribute of a thoughtless superior, though unfortunately most common. The only thing such punitive actions achieve is providing an outlet to irrational anger. The few situations that warrant punishment due to negligence, the scope of deploying punishment intelligently for changing or improving behaviour or performance is drastically reduced. The lesson is: don't blast impulsively. Think about the possible causes of inadequate performance. If the mistake is due to negligence, and you don't reprimand or punish, you are encouraging its repetition: if it was not within his capabilities or experience, don't punish him for it, when, in fact, it shows your poor judgement. Most people are in the habit of lashing out, without first analysing the situation.

THE PUNISHED FEEL VICTIMIZED, NOT MOTIVATED TO CHANGE

The other dreadful consequence of a reprimand is that while you feel your subordinate has done something wrong, he is, most probably, far from convinced. And unless he feels that he is in the wrong, he is going to find your criticism unfair, and feel uncomfortable or even miserable. He would feel that being the boss, you are throwing your weight around, and he is being victimized unfairly. He might start feeling that the boss is letting out his pent-up aggression. These, we would recall, are defense mechanisms and we have learnt in earlier chapters that no change is possible till defense mechanisms actively operate. People react to frustration in different ways, deploying

The other dreadful consequence of a reprimand is that while you feel your subordinate has done something wrong, he is, most probably, far from convinced. And unless he feels that he is in the wrong, he is going to find your criticism unfair, and feel uncomfortable or even miserable. He would feel that being the boss, you are throwing your weight around, and he is being victimized unfairly.

different defense mechanisms, based on their predispositions. Some subordinates, for instance, might become aggressive and resist, if not revolt. Others might get depressed in the face of helpless situations (being blamed unnecessarily though they feel they are doing their best), and some might become cynical. (In this organization, doing good or real hardwork is pointless, it is never appreciated). The fact is that very few superiors first find out how receptive the subordinate is or whether he is convinced about his fault, before they vent their impulsive reactions or frustration. Our earlier learning in establishing trustworthy relations *before* even attempting improvements could be deployed here most relevantly. The thrust of the argument is that in most situations, people are not convinced about the fault they are being accused of. A superior must first win the confidence of a subordinate before he blames or reprimands. The outbursts or even mere disapproval in a majority of cases just boomerangs. This takes us to another limitation of the effectiveness of punishment.

PUNISHMENT DOESN'T TEACH THE RIGHT WAY OR HOW TO DO BETTER

A punished person, at best, learns what not to do or how not to do something. It does not indicate what needs to be done and how to do it. Do you often find the person being reprimanded confused about what he should have done to get different results? While reinforcing rewarded behaviour clearly indicates what to do the next time or what is expected of the person being rewarded, punishment leaves one in the dark about what is desired of a person or how should he get it.

USE OF HARSH INSTEAD OF MILD PUNISHMENT

Researches have confirmed that mild punishments are more effective than harsh ones. Yet many of us use the latter, hoping to achieve quick or better results. A harsh punishment, it is assumed, will be remembered for a longer time or will remain effective for long time to come. Mild punishments are less likely to rouse feelings of resentment and thus, they are more effective in moulding behaviour.

SEVERE PUNISHMENTS FOR SEVERE BLUNDERS?

Major faults or blunders are usually dealt with severely. The assumption often is deterrence, i.e. only harsh punishment would scare a person or prevent him from repeating an act. Common sense dictates that big blunders or wrongs justify harsh punishment. If that was so, researches have shown that the number of murders taking place in countries that have abolished capital punishment would be more than in countries that have not abolished the death sentence. Official data compiled over the decades by various countries negate this belief. Punishments of mountainous magnitude are not needed to bring about changes in individuals. Small things said or explained in subtle ways could also lead to magnanimous developments. A single match can become a burning inferno; being thrown out from a train transformed Gandhi into Mahatma...

Scientific evidence and everyday observations do not support the belief that harsh punishment is more effective in changing people, though they provide false justification of meeting justice. Harsh punishments do, however, turn the relationships sour forever, breaking them beyond repair:

AT TIMES, IT IS BEST NOT TO PUNISH AT ALL

After the subordinate has made a serious mistake, call him, discuss the issue with him to make him understand what he has done. If you find him remorseful, it's enough that you have made him realize the mistake. I would go to the extent of suggesting that give him a similar assignment when feasible, and just tell him that this time you hope he would show that he is capable of doing a good job. Be sure, this time, he will really put in his best, because he has much more to prove himself and erase his 'incompetent' image. If he succeeds in doing so, you are assured that you also have succeeded in bringing about in him the change which you were seeking.

SKILLS OF REPRIMANDING

Having reviewed the limitations and *when to punish*, let us now focus on the skills required for punishing or *how to punish*, reprimand or be critical to get the best results. If something has disappointed or annoyed you, whether at home or work, it is necessary to give expression to your feelings. If it is at home, the chances are you have been hurt emotionally due to the nature of your relationships with the people involved. Keeping the feelings pent-up will not only sour your relationship, but also keep you agitated, and hurt you health in the long run. At office, you not only have to develop your juniors, producing quality work output, but also retain friendly and trusting relationships with your people, all of which would be seriously affected if you stayed silent for long. After analysing whether the act of omission or commission was due to negligence or because it was beyond one's capabilities, whether one would feel victimized or be receptive to feedback, reprimand using these principles and procedure.

BE FRANK, BUT FIRM AND COOL

Unless you find it impossible to control your temper because of one's highly inexcusable behaviour, better wait for a day or two to talk to one about it. Tell him frankly why you are upset, point out his mistake, and what, in your view, are its consequences. Be straightforward, don't mince your words but stay cool. Most importantly, make very sure that you do not become judgemental to begin with; do not forget that you still have to find the reason for his behaviour. It is very important to remember one of the three principles we covered earlier to create trust. The lesser the judgemental words used, the more receptive he would be to introspect and share the details. But if you become judgemental and criticize him at the outset, you have lost the opportunity of doing any good or getting the desired results. Do everything, therefore, to allow him to open up.

BE PRECISE AND SPECIFIC, NEVER GENERALIZE

Speak about what was wrong with reference to specific actions or events. Never ever generalize: 'You always do that...', 'That time also...' and 'That day also...'. You would give him the impression that you have now turned against him, especially if you keep criticizing him for one thing after the other. Never take up all the previous episodes which call for punishment at the same time or together.

NEVER USE ADJECTIVES

Never use adjectives like lazy, inefficient, careless, etc. You will threaten his self-esteem, image and vanity. As we learnt in an earlier chapter, defense mechanisms nullify the efforts to change. Not only will the efforts go futile, but you will create mutual hostilities.

Should you do any of above mentioned mistakes (use adjectives or switch criticism from what happened on one occasion to another, from his one weakness to the other), have no doubt that you have conveyed the message that for some reason, you have turned against him, or are now settling scores with him (though you might not be really be doing or intending that). Therefore, never make the mistake of postponing the criticism which you feel is justified, with a view that on some appropriate occasion, you will take it up all together. It is a common blunder; avoid it at any cost.

ENSURE THAT THE TIMING IS RIGHT

The exception to the rule of delivering rewards and punishments *immediately*, is the state of mind. If he is in a dejected or aggressive mood, or is recovering from a recent unpleasant episode or encounter—especially with you—even your well-intended communication will result in further depression, cynicism, retaliation or, at best, getting ignored. Check out the timing first, because a receptive or positive frame of mind significantly enhances the probability of the feedback or suggestion succeeding in bringing about the change in him. Apart from his mood and mental setup, your own predisposition is important. Never appear to be in a hurry or hard-pressed for time when you are giving feedback or mentoring. Being in a hurry conveys that you are not in charge of things or your own self. Retaining a relaxed and cool posture would convey your confidence in your capacity to manage the issues at hand.

To sum up the discussion on punishment:

By being frank but non-judgemental, not digging into or linking the current issue with the past, and not using adjectives, you would enable him to open up the gates for you so that you could play the role of a change agent. Punishment is legitimate, if the performance deficit resulted from negligence, and he realizes his role in it.

MANAGING BY FEAR OF NON-PERFORMANCE

During seminars, I have conducted on 'leading', 'inspiring' and 'developing' people, participants have often commented that for achieving higher degree of task-orientation, the fear of punishment for non-performance is really essential, because in the absence of such a fear, people tend to take it easy and are nonchalant about the task assigned. People-orientation—empathy, etc., does not produce good results in their experience. Is that your experience too? Do you feel that in the absence of any fear, people tend to be callous in their work? This is a frequently discussed subject.

Your experience could be valid in some cases, but watch out for two important consequences in all cases, if you are managing people by creating in them the fear of the consequences of non-performance.

First, since people are performing under the fear of being caught for sub-standard performance, the obvious implication is that should you withdraw even if for a while, from close supervision that you need to spot any flaw in their work, they also will withdraw their involvement in work till you get back to overseeing their work again. And if they are working under fear, you must not take a break from supervision even for a short while, so as to keep them in the grip of fear. This can result in you tiring yourself endlessly. Instead of attending to your other duties, you will exhaust yourself due to constant supervision.

Once I was speaking to the Commissioner of Police during the programme on this very subject for senior IPS officers, and enquired how police officers inspired their deputies to raise the standard of their performance. I was not surprised when he mentioned that getting work done in police was never a problem because they have to work under a strict disciplinary regime and carry out the commands of their seniors. I was, however, astonished to find that it never occurred to the Commissioner that those who work under pressure or fear will deliver only what is specifically asked for, and will never achieve anything on their own by taking initiative, exercising free will or creativity. For instance, while undertaking investigations to solve a problem, they might not bother about any promising leads suddenly surfacing and take on more work, because their boss, not aware about those leads, never asked them to work on them. If their work is merely to carry out the command, why should they use their own initiative or creativity or add on extra work that is not part of the 'orders'?

The second highly avoidable consequence of such a managing style is the poor quality of output. The assumption underlying managing people by fear is that they are unlikely to use their initiative and will focus on completing what they have been specifically told to do, so that they are not penalized. They will churn out minimum work, which will be of the lowest quality—which indeed appears to be unfortunately true in many bureaucratic organizations. Organizations practising such a managing style are likely to suffer from developing a competitive edge and from poor public image. Such a supervisor or leader will never get the best his people can produce; he will get only what he asked for and in the manner he asked them to go about doing it. Producing high-quality creative work necessarily calls for freedom and initiative on part of all involved.

To summarize, even while some astute professionals believe that fear has a place in obtaining performance, the style of creating fear for inadequate performance is flawed as it could lead to two very damaging consequences. One, close and constant supervision is required to ensure that subordinates know that their lapses will be spotted, which becomes tiring for the supervisor, who in addition gets little time for attending to his other tasks. Two, the superior would get minimum work and poor-quality output, just 'passable' and at the most, what was asked for.

The style of creating fear for inadequate performance is flawed as it could lead to two very damaging consequences. One, close and constant supervision is required to ensure that subordinates know that their lapses will be spotted, which becomes tiring for the supervisor, who in addition gets little time for attending to his other tasks. Two, the superior would get minimum work and poor-quality output, just 'passable' and at the most, what was asked for.

MAKE THEM FEEL IMPORTANT

I know one very competent professional who was working as General Manager—Marketing, and had burnt the midnight oil for his company, preparing a presentation which his boss, Director—Marketing, had to make to company directors during their annual planning exercise. Though at number two, everyone in the company knew that he was the number one talent in the organization, without whom the strategic plan could not be developed. Since I was instrumental in putting him in that organization, he came to tell me how he had felt hurt by the deeds of the director and decided to leave the company. He related to me how he had been snubbed by the director for whose sake he had slogged, when he happened to make some innocent enquiry. 'You don't bother about it. That is the top management matter and we shall think about it', was the reply he got from his boss.

This might be a rather extreme example, but you might have heard certain bosses snubbing their subordinates with similar comments: 'You won't understand it', 'You don't bother about it' or 'This is a prerogative of the top management', etc. Though what we are discussing here is how to inspire people, I thought I should briefly mention this as one of the best ways of killing people's inspiration. Let us understand that the superior has nothing to gain (except perhaps some false pride), but everything to lose by belittling his own people. A good leader will invariably do the opposite: boost their ego, tell them that he considered them and their contribution invaluable to the company.

Explain to your people how their work is important

A person who takes pride in his work is capable of putting in much higher effort to produce the best results he is capable of, as compared to the one whom you have made to feel insignificant.

for the growth and functioning of the organization. Tell a 'lowly' accountant how the accuracy and timely reports are so important for the top management to take correct decisions. Now, watch the difference in his performance. Tell your 'ordinary' manufacturing chemist how his contribution to the maintenance of quality of the products is the backbone of the organization's fortune, and watch the change in his attitude towards work.

Here is an inspirational strategy to get good results. A person who takes pride in his work is capable of putting in much higher effort to produce the best results he is capable of, as compared to the one whom you have made to feel insignificant.

REWARD GOOD BEHAVIOUR, INSTEAD OF PERFORMANCE

Many promoters, especially in India, are acclaimed for managing their organizations like an extended family. While mercifully, this trend is reducing, one element of such management practice seems to prevail, consciously or not, somewhat more widely. It is the tendency of promoters and bosses to reward good behaviour instead of performance. This is what parents do to children. Therefore, when some people start behaving too politely or obsequiously, anticipating and fulfilling the personal needs of their superiors, they evoke admiration, at times even increments and promotions, from their bosses. This results in multiple damages. For work organization must produce results (not decent guys) for its sheer survival, and if you reward behaviour on the basis of your likes and dislikes, you might develop sycophants (bent on pleasing you any how), but not a performing organization.

The culture in such an organization gives birth to the belief that what really matters in the organization is how close you are to the bosses, or whether you are in their good books or not. Worst, you will demotivate the real performers, who would opt out for some other organization, as they are less interested in pleasing the boss.

As said, though the practice of managing organizations like extended families is fast disappearing, the tendency to reward those who are particularly nice is not so difficult to explain. It is very difficult not to be nice to those who are nice to you. They fulfil important psychological needs of the superiors; they make them feel they are wanted, boost their self-image and provide precious oxygen to their ego. It's only human to reward such people. But unless these tendencies are brought under control, they would prove damaging to the organization, and also to the long-term career of the one who learns to rely on his good behaviour in lieu of performance.

YOU WILL GET WHAT YOU ASK FOR

By and large, people tend to meet the expectations you have from them. If you convey to your subordinates that your expectations are pretty high, chances are that they would deliver them to you, or at least do more than what they would have otherwise done. But if they get the message—overtly or covertly—that you, in any case, don't expect much from them, you should be more or less sure that they would be delighted to prove you right. So, don't leave your expectations unsaid. Convey to them emphatically and with conviction that you expect them to perform better than earlier, even if the job looks formidable. Should they complete the job satisfactorily, the next thing you do is even more important. Give them a bigger and more challenging assignment, stating it in a confident manner that you are confident that it is within their capabilities to do it. I do not think there can be a better method of preparing people for higher responsibilities and positions than to stretch their capabilities on increasingly challenging assignments and watch them perform. Often, this would call for the trust in the capabilities in one's mentees and in few cases undertaking some risk, but this will ultimately help you and their development as well. Nothing should, of course, ever be exaggerated, not even gospel truths, I believe. However, it would be reasonable to say that more often than not, whether you think they can do it or not, you are right. Your own optimism too, would contribute a great deal, though the expectations that you have conveyed would move your subordinates to meet them with the thrust required. All this is based on the assumption that you share a good equation i.e. they like to work for you. And that is why it is important to develop trust, before anything else.

LOYALTY IS LIABILITY

With economic and cultural transitions taking rapid strides, the concept of loyalty is fortunately being left behind—at least in more progressive organizations. I know this thought would appear a bit too unconventional and radical, or even shock some, but this is not a mere hypothesis. It is based on my empirical observations, during my long consulting practice and as a leadership coach to CEOs and promoters. If large

If you convey to your subordinates your high expectations, chances are that they would complete the task or at least do more than what they would have otherwise done. However, more often than not, your judgement about whether they can do it or not is right.

number of bosses still admire and reward loyalty, the reasons are not too difficult to trace. Psychologically, loyalty is often accompanied by liking and desire to seek proximity with the boss, and most bosses, therefore, take it as a compliment and love it. It thrives on the foundation of an emotional bond—real, imagined or desired.

I believe that those who had consciously cultivated loyalties and the admiration of their people (or if loyalties were the result of subordinates' liking for their bosses), had created subordinates who had become dependent in thought and action (or decision-making). They were eager to please the boss by adhering to even his stereotype 'model behaviour' which was evolved based on their perception of what he liked, how he talked and dressed, and other such personal preferences. This, they hoped, though not always consciously, will win them accolades and thus gratify their needs of getting closer to him. A lot of a superior's time gets wasted by the subordinates trying to meet him on one pretext or the other, but in reality to gratify the psychological needs that the superiors had created in the subordinates. These 'loyal' employees failed to develop the degree of independence required to be an effective manager, leave alone that of a leader. The boss, too, in his eagerness to please them, rewarded them not so much on merit but with a view to retain their loyalties. The superiors who create a band of loyalists unknowingly getting into the situation of the 'after-me' deluge, apart from other serious consequences like not getting time to do their job or developing the enterprise. This sort of loyalty, which is becoming a liability, is being increasingly replaced by a professional equation (or unwritten professional contract) in enlightened organizations. Such an equation of

Those who had consciously cultivated loyalties and the admiration of their people (or if loyalties were the result of subordinates' liking for their bosses), had created subordinates who had become dependent in thought and action (or decision-making).

These 'loyal' employees failed to develop the degree of independence required to be an effective manager and they left little time for their superiors to attend to their own priorities.

understanding, though not fully devoid of human component, works to the advantage of all concerned. The professional contract implies that he contributes to the company and in return, the company to him: the more he contributes to the growth of the company, the more the company will do for him. It, therefore, becomes fair on the part of the boss to expect the best from his people, because the company provides them the avenues to fulfil the wide spectrum of needs they live for: pay hikes, promotion and status, a sense of achievement and even his personal growth to his fullest potential and satisfaction. In this fair and just system, neither the boss nor his people could ask for more!

The concept of loyalty was very appropriate in the earlier feudal society. But in the current era of economic growth that offers plenty of opportunities, especially in knowledge-based industries, it is better we usher into contemporary systems and practices. Fortunately, superiors, subordinates and organizations, all gain a lot by basing their relationships on professional and reciprocal expectations, as long as it is not totally devoid of human factor which is always involved in all sorts of human relationships.

USE AMBITIOUS SELF-SEEKERS TO ACHIEVE BIG ORGANIZATIONAL GOALS

Having given up the concept of personal loyalty, abandon organizational loyalty too!

We have heard so many organizational bosses affirming that they don't want overambitious, selfish, self-seekers in their organizations. But I think you should consider yourself

The exceptionally ambitious manifest the energy of erupting volcanoes, which they harness fully. Just three or four of them will achieve as much as twenty others having moderate ambition.

lucky if you do have few such ambitious, self-seekers in the organization. In my own small consulting setup, my selection process was geared to searching out these self-seekers, ambitious (but, of course, capable) people, and I benefited immensely by this strategy. The exceptionally ambitious manifest the energy of erupting volcanoes, which they harness fully. You just have to make sure that you convey to them—and ensure that they are convinced that their personal ambitions, i.e. their driving force—can be gratified in *your* organization, if they produce exceptional results. To lead these people for getting the best results, just ensure two things: (a) guide them to channelize their energies and make them consistent with organizational priorities, (b) never fail to reward them as soon as they achieve something significant. The latter is necessary, or they will stop believing that they are in right organization and start seeking out other opportunities, where they could climb up faster. Prove to them that the organization rewards good performance, always. That will keep them on track; the more motivated they are, the more the benefits that will be reaped by the organization. Once you have convinced these ambitious self-seekers that your organization is the right place for them to fulfil their dreams, just three or four of them will achieve as much as twenty others having moderate ambition.

FOCUS ON INDIVIDUALS; THEY ARE MORE IMPORTANT THAN TEAMS

People take to fads very fast, and, unfortunately, this is particularly true of professionals in the field of management. Any new concept or practice that appears on the scene, and we start believing that a panacea has been invented to take care of all our ailments. 'Teamwork' is one such mantra everyone seems to be reciting in all organizations.

Teamwork is not always the best approach and could indeed prove much less productive if it dilutes the focus of an individual (which, unfortunately, it does). There are many reasons for this.

First, the output of even a very cohesive team would not always be the sum total of the output of its individuals, if they were to be led and inspired separately. The slower understanding or low productivity of one team member could hamper both, quality and quantity of work. Team norms could very often be the source of frustration for highly ambitious and competent individuals who could produce more but will not, because of the group pressure for compliance with the group standards, which are lower. In our overenthusiasm to embrace new concepts, we often forget the old time-tested studies including the ones on 'norm busters', which are valid even now.

Second, teamwork is important when work is interdependent, i.e. a work-flow chart shows that it cannot be completed without cooperation or involvement of two or more people. However, the fact is that work is not always interdependent, so everyone's effectiveness does not depend on group productivity. Many jobs are not interdependent on others, and individuals could produce results without the expertise of others. For instance, the job of the manager in-charge of working capital who deals with banks for financial accommodation, corporate planning and most typically, of salespersons or sales engineers, each of whom works

Teamwork is not always the best approach in various situations and could indeed prove unproductive if it dilutes the focus of an individual (which, unfortunately, it does).

The individuals, in any case, are the basic units of what comprises a team (physical reality as against an abstract 'team'). Their own driving forces are highly potent in determining group norms, as much as their own output, and they also act as the fuel supply of the teams they are part of.

independently or have been allotted jurisdictions or territories. In fact, instead of team spirit or cooperation, the competition created among the sales personnel with the reward to the highest performer enhances the performance of the whole group.

Thirdly, while the team has the capacity to satisfy some individual needs (like affiliative, or bonding), it frustrates more of them (need for power, recognition and individual attainment). We have already discussed the importance of harnessing and managing highly ambitious individuals, few of whom, when properly managed, could equal the performance of many moderately ambitious. Focusing on the recognition and achievement of the team instead of individuals would result in the organization loosing many ambitious executives.

Lastly, teams often have to evolve or work with standarized procedures and practices to perform the task they have been entrusted. This would dampen the individual urges of experimentation and creativity—invaluable for some individuals, but even more for the organization.

It is not my intention to throw away a baby with the tub water. I too, hold the view that teamwork is indispensable when the work of certain individuals is interdependent or if the work technology demands it. However, whether you intend to raise organizational performance by focusing on an individual or the team, I think the strategies of leading people based on the needs and driving forces of individuals are likely to bring far better results. This is because individuals, in any case, are the basic units of what comprises a team (the physical reality as against an abstract 'team'), and their driving forces are highly potent in determining group norms, as much as their own output, and they also act as the fuel supply of the teams they are part of.

DEVELOP A DEEPER INSIGHT INTO
THE DYNAMICS OF DELEGATION

You really have no choice but to delegate. And you also know that delegation is not a way of passing the buck. You alone remain responsible for the results whether or not you delegate or whether it works or not. Successful delegation, however, depends on many factors. Entire books have been devoted exclusively to this subject. I, therefore, intend on highlighting just a few factors which, I believe, have not received the attention they deserve, though are crucially important in determining the success or failure of delegation. I shall divide these factors into three categories: those within a superior or leader; those within subordinates; and those in the process of delegating itself.

Factors within the superior

Apart from the confidence you have in subordinates, what and how much you delegate will, I guess, depend upon three psychological factors within you. First, your personal needs. Those with stronger personal power drive (and incidentally, there is nothing bad about it) are more comfortable with directing and giving detailed instructions about the job that needs to be carried out; others not so comfortable with using power and considering it unfair to overtly display their power or authority tend to take a more interactive approach, sharing their thoughts, encouraging participation, and letting the juniors decide. But if you are a former personality type, you might not be getting much benefits of delegating, as you might be wasting too much time in giving directions and supervising.

The second factor that could substantially reduce the benefits of delegation is the 'perfectionist' tendency among superiors. Don't forget that it is better to get ten projects done even if they fall 10 per cent short of your 'perfectionist' standards than to have one project done in the same time, no matter how perfect. And in most cases, the effort and time required for achieving about 100 per cent perfection is probably twice more than that required for completing anything that is 90 per cent. Is it worth being a perfectionist and always be behind schedule in most projects? The suggestion, therefore, is that do not stop delegating due to fear that your subordinates will not deliver 100 per cent results you want and remain laid-back. Instead, be pragmatic and achieve more.

Finally, it is your anxiety level or the tolerance of the uncertainty of the outcome that determines how much you delegate. It is well established that more confident and self-assured people delegate far more than those who are anxiety prone and less secure.

Forces within subordinates

The personality and the needs of the subordinates must naturally be factored into by the superior who delegates. Elsewhere in the book, we have already discussed that the fundamental research that I had carried out, has shown that the *dependence need*—the important and relevant variable in this context—is not uni-dimentional. It is of two types: work dependence (shown in seeking detailed work instructions) and emotional dependence on superior (shown in seeking physical and emotional proximity and bonding with the superior). Unlike the prevailing belief, research cited earlier had shown that these two needs are totally different or independent of each other. These findings also have major implications for the process of delegation. It implies that the superior must know that even by giving freedom in their work, he does not abdicate his responsibility for the emotional gratification of the needs of some subordinates. He might give them full freedom in work, but he should keep meeting them, to retain the personal bond. Conversely, the superior must know which subordinates prefer to keep their personal relations aloof, and confine themselves to work relations, which covers getting all the guidance, help and directions. Leading and delegating become much more effective when based on this understanding of the dynamics of the subordinacy or need-driven behaviour of reportees.

Forces in the delegation process

Coming to the process of delegation, clarify what and how much you are delegating; let no ambiguity remain. This will help you avoid any resentment from your subordinates and will ensure that you are all on the same page. This will also ensure that work, functions, the decision-making authority and deadlines are clearly spelt out and the organizational goals are met in time.

Delegating 'correctly' is a very important part of developing and leading people. You must, therefore, carefully analyse your own drives, the characteristics of your subordinates and your delegating process, if you want to derive all the benefits of delegating properly, i.e. use the expertise and skills of others

Success in delegating is determined by three factors. if you want to derive all the benefits of delegating properly, you must carefully analyse: your own drives or characteristics; that of your subordinates'; and your delegating process.

to save your time and energy, and achieve better results for yourself.

DON'T CREATE A SERIOUS ATMOSPHERE
TO GET HIGHER PERFORMANCE

Just because work is serious business, it does not mean that you have to look, act or behave seriously all the time. A stiff and stern attitude, especially during long and continuous work sessions, is not essential for carrying out the work conscientiously and with full involvement. Inject some lighter moments with wit, humour, or a joke in long and continuous work. If that does not come naturally, just call for a coffee break. Lighten the atmosphere only in a way that is natural to you. And just because you are the boss or leader, it does not make it obligatory that you have to take up the role of being witty and humorous yourself (it's quite funny incidentally, that practically all of us mistakenly believe ourselves to be witty and humorous). Let someone else do this job during the coffee break.

Such fun-filled mini-breaks have many advantages. One: Fun has the potential to lift the boredom, tension and fatigue that comes with long-drawn sessions. It, as if magically, makes a person feel at ease and relaxed. At the physical level, there is a revival of energy, and on the psychological front, moods are elevated. Everyone in the group feels energized, physically as well as mentally. It is a great antidote to tension and fatigue.

Second: Fatigue and boredom are not conducive to creativity and productivity, ease and relaxation are. When one gets back to work after a while, one is not only fresh and rejuvenated, but potentially more creative and productive. The team then churns out more and better ideas.

Third: Such interactions lead to bonding, cohesiveness and an enhanced team spirit.

Whenever boredom, fatigue or ennui set in, especially during long working sessions, infusing some fun and lighter moments is not being frivolous in your work; it is for productivity and bonding.

MAKE NO FALSE PROMISES: IT'S HIGHLY DEMOTIVATING

An important point, though it does not need much elaboration. I have observed many times during my consulting career, that when some superiors or organizational leaders are pleased with some act of their subordinates, they instantaneously promise: 'You will take over as senior manager in a few months', 'You will take over from so and so, very soon', 'You will get the highest increment next time, I will commend you to the big boss', etc. I have seen this happen often. As it happens, it becomes difficult to keep such promises for various reasons: policy or procedural constraints, impact which such actions would have on others, which you had not thought through, etc. Few things demotivate as much as the frustration of living with an unkept promise.

Don't ever forget that people will soon start judging you based on the promises you have kept. You could lose people's trust and the value of your words if they start sharing their experiences of how you have been making promises without meaning to keep them.

Keep in mind your capability and authority on acting on

Few things demotivate as much as the frustration of living with an unkept promise.

the promises you make. In case you are dependent on others to act on your promises like your seniors, moderate your lofty promises. Convey to your subordinate only what you can do and what you really will. In fact, you will still retain their goodwill for being perceived as helpful and concerned about them. If you are the senior-most person, it is even more important that you never act impulsively in announcing rewards, before you have deliberated on various implications of living up with your promises.

TRYING TIMES IN AN ORGANIZATION DEMAND ALTERNATIVE STYLES AND STRATEGIES

The type of response or output you want from your subordinates depends on the objectives of the organization. The strategies or how you get the output depends on your own needs and skills and that of your subordinates. However, there are times when exigencies alone determine how you get results, no matter what your needs or usual style of managing is. This could happen if the organization faces the danger of survival. During such times, you have to ignore the virtues of people-orientation, participative styles or high-end strategies, and adopt a rather ruthless, work-oriented approach to ensure the survival of the organization. This could, for instance, mean sacking people, freezing their salaries, etc. Another situation could be a shift in the life cycle of the organization. The initial or pioneering stage of the organization often compels you to make your executives run like 'chhokras' or errand boys, as the focus is on getting things done and getting the operations started. At a later stage, as the organization matures, when the system and practices are in place, executives should be given respect and freedom to run the organization. The strategies you need to lead and inspire people are, therefore, different at different life stages of an organization.

The critical question you must answer yourself is whether you are capable of playing these two roles, often contradictory in two situations (for instance, dictatorial vs participative, work vs emotional concern, etc.), and still be in one piece? The truth is that very few can. History illustrates that even presidents or prime ministers who were good during war time, were generally not successful at peace time and vice versa. The dilemma you have to work out is whether you could be flexible enough to take on the role you probably have so far not played—or is inherently incompatible with what you are—or to quit. These are the trying times: either they are great opportunities that bring to the surface your hidden strengths and you come out as winner; or it's time you leave, to avoid failure, its mental agony and its lurking shadow on you and your future. How far your inherent nature which determines your natural way of leading people is compatible with the style of leading required by an organization at a particular time, is the question you must ask and answer yourself, after some honest introspection.

KEEP COMMUNICATING AND CREATING TRUST

Having discussed strategies for changing, mentoring and developing, let us go back to the thought we started with. Meet informally once in a while and keep communicating. Do not stop personal communication even on the excellent pretext given by many in senior management that they manage by delegating fully, or by getting all the information they need through an excellent information system, and deploying modern technology, or the likes. I have so often heard senior executives boasting that they don't have to spend much time going to factories or various other divisions to meet people and know what is happening. Data and systems, no matter how effective, do not develop any bond between you and your people, whom you must keep charged all the time so that they give their best. As you keep communicating, you will develop mutual trust and an equation, which, as this book has maintained, is the mandatory requirement for inspiring, developing and mentoring people. They are never open to you if they cannot trust you, or if the personal equation is absent. There is no substitute to personal touch.

FINALLY, DON'T LET DEMOTIVATION SPREAD

You have made the earnest and sincere effort to apply all the techniques, tools and strategies discussed here. Are you still left with some tough nut to crack? Less probable, but in such an exceptional case, do not permit just one rotten apple to spoil the whole basket. Say good-bye and eject the tough nut to save the system (if yours is a government or such organization that does not sack people, make sure to put him on some inconsequential job where he cannot do any damage to the organization). You might not always be able to identify him through any vocalized doubts or disagreements, which he is unlikely to express, but you could probably catch him in the 'loo', talking cynically with his colleagues, neutralizing all your efforts and intentions to raise the bar of the performance of your people. But make sure that after ejecting him or putting him in his place, you retain all the conviction and zeal to practise all the strategies and techniques again, building them on a foundation of trust by deploying the process of influence for enhancing performance and relationships with people.

Epilogue
Who and How Much to Mentor

DON'T PUSH TOO HARD: TO SUCCEED, KNOW YOUR LIMITS

I saw my friend scold his driver and I asked him the reason for his rage. 'This person is in the habit of lying. I shall see to it that he quits lying,' he said. I looked at the man. He appeared to me about fifty-five years old. Was it possible for him to change now? Or was my friend hitting his head against the wall? Lying is a type of defense mechanism, usually aimed at protecting oneself or someone else from some fear or insecurity. Before my friend did it, probably hundred others must have reprimanded him for it. His habit will leave him perhaps when his deep-seated insecurities are pulled out of his system, where they are firmly entrenched. This was a job to be assigned to a competent professional.

One so often hears superiors admonishing their subordinates to 'act more intelligently'. This undermines the intelligence of the boss who innocently is assuming that people act or project themselves as morons deliberately. Or advising people while mentoring them not to sit at home, but spend evenings networking with clients and professionals in their field to achieve success. This, though, usually is the prerogative of wives who keep goading their husbands not to sit at home in the evening with books or drinks while relaxing with soothing music, and instead accompany them on hopping trips to clubs, friends, etc. In both the situations, the aim is to transform an introvert into an extrovert—neither possible nor desirable. This ends up as an effort totally wasted. Worse, it leads to rifts or arguments. Not just that; the fact is that these enduring personality characteristics impart people their unique identity –an 'extrovert' against an 'introvert'. Prudence demands that we fully appreciate the wealth and richness in diversity, which is the essence of mankind. A mentor or change agent must eschew attempts to demolish or radically change anyone's unique identity. Nor should he imagine that he himself is the ideal person or an idol to be envied. Realizing the importance of diversity in thinking and behaviour of people is the sign of maturity in a person who is playing the role of a developer or a mentor.

So what is a boss or anyone—whether spouse, parent or friend—interested in changing and helping people, trying to achieve? Firstly, the objective should be specific and worthy of the efforts. It cannot be an 'overall' improvement or being a clone of the boss ('I will develop him to be like me', a very common, though horrible boast of deluded bosses) or someone, no matter how worthy of emulation. The right to be different is guaranteed by nature itself. Secondly, and more importantly, the mentor or change agent should have the capability to achieve that objective. And this is what the second part of the book was about: how to develop capabilities of becoming a successful change agent, developer or mentor, and enhance the performance of people while simultaneously improving your relationships with them. Yet, not everyone has the 'inherent' capabilities to imbibe and practise them fully, and mentors will always have different calibre to change and mentor. *A successful or an insightful mentor would usually attempt only such changes which are within his competence to achieve.*

DON'T WORK ON THE UNWILLING, THOUGH YOU MAY INSPIRE AND PLAN STRATEGICALLY

You want to change and develop your subordinates so that you could show results and raise your stock value in the company. You want to change your spouse most probably because you want to have an upper hand and have your way. You want to change your domestic help so that she/he learns what you need and make your life comfortable. You want your child to change in a way so that he grows up into the person you want to see in him/her and perhaps to fulfil your unfulfilled dreams. And you thought this book will help you how to get this all, i.e. change the people your way. NO WAY! This is because of the reasons why *you* want them to change. Unless they are motivated and convinced about why they should and can bring about the change that you want, you neither have any power nor strategies to bring enduring changes in them. You cannot change one who does not want to change, or change him to something or someone that he does not like to be.

But should you not try to change a person, even if he/she is unwilling to change, to help him for instance realize his full potential, which is in his own interest; or even in mutual interest (e.g., spouse for sake of better adjustment), even though he/she was unwilling or resisted the change? In the first part of the book, we discussed why people resist change: perceived uncertainty (of the outcome) and non-acceptance of one's inadequacies (character/capabilities). Creating trust, it would be pertinent to recall, is the first condition to change, mentor or develop people, and which is why the way to create trust was elaborately discussed. ('Strategies', the focus of the second part of the book, was the other pre-requisite). However, even if the trust between the two exists or has been created, we just established that one ought not to attempt changing anyone for personal or selfish reasons, or transforming anyone into someone else, no matter how adorable. This was because of the unacceptable intentions behind mentoring. Now assuming that the mentor is competent, trust exists, and there are no ulterior motives at work, a generic question of wider interest is yet to be addressed: *Should one try or is it prudent to try and change an unwilling person, even if it is in his own interests?*

In my view, if change or development results in mutual, instead of selfish or ideological gain, or benefits the individual being 'helped', it is a legitimate endeavour. Changing the unwilling, even when the motive is unselfish, however, will succeed only if a few crucial initial steps are undertaken before following rest of the process of mentoring covered in the book. In other words, one has to prepare the ground for the unmotivated or the unwilling, and then follow the usual approaches common to all. 'Preparing the ground' involves achieving two specific goals.

First, it is important to convert one's unwillingness or apathy into not just interest, but zealousness and enthusiasm. How do you do that? Describe the goal or outcome. Help him visualize the outcome: point out to him the chair or cabin of the boss, which he would be occupying if he achieves the required development; to your son, tell him how he can become more successful than you and have a better house, better car and more luxurious holidays; to your wife, help her with visualizing the hope of reliving the nostalgic memory she has of the honey-moon days, and so on... Put the outcome or result of the effort very positively, not forgetting that abstract words are a poor substitute of the positive *visualization* in terms of their motivational pull. Visualizing is better than verbalizing. Visualize the outcome jointly with him/her not once but often, till he/she finds himself/herself really lured by the goal and agrees to make a commitment.

However, the lure of the goal alone is not enough to get the commitment. He has to feel confident that the outcome sought is within his reach or capabilities. The second step, therefore, is to assure him that he has the capability to realize the goal. In addition to giving him confidence in his capabilities to achieve the goal, a mentor must assure him that he would also be available to assist and guide him, if he could. However lured he might feel towards the goal, without confidence in his capabilities to reach the goal or belief that its achievable, the motivation will surely sag soon.

These are, therefore, two pre-requisites for changing and developing people who are unwilling or indifferent. First, tap their fantasies and dreams and help them *visualize* their dreams coming true. The dreams and fantasies surely create more motivation and zeal to achieve than intellect or analytical calibre. Secondly, create in him the confidence that the goal is within his capabilities to achieve. But if your repartee is not consciously resisting his development, you could straightaway use these approaches to leading and mentoring, to benefit you, your people, and the organization.